Diary 2016

F

FRANCES LINCOLN LIMITED

PUBLISHERS

Frances Lincoln Limited
www.franceslincoln.com

The British Library Desk Diary 2016
Copyright © Frances Lincoln Limited 2015
Images and text © The British Library 2015

Astronomical information © Crown Copyright.
Reproduced by permission of the Controller of
Her Majesty's Stationery Office and the UK
Hydrographic Office (www.ukho.gov.uk)

A catalogue record for this book is available
from the British Library

Designed by Arianna Osti

ISBN: 9780711236394

Printed and bound in China

TITLE PAGE **Drink Me**, illustration by Sir John Tenniel, London, 1890.
[Cup.410.g.74]

BELOW **The Queen's Croquet-Ground** and ABOVE **Cheshire Cat**,
illustrations by Gwynedd M. Hudson, London, 1922. [YA.1997.b.4119]

2016

JANUARY
M T W T F S S
```
            1  2  3
 4  5  6  7  8  9 10
11 12 13 14 15 16 17
18 19 20 21 22 23 24
25 26 27 28 29 30 31
```

FEBRUARY
M T W T F S S
```
 1  2  3  4  5  6  7
 8  9 10 11 12 13 14
15 16 17 18 19 20 21
22 23 24 25 26 27 28
29
```

MARCH
M T W T F S S
```
    1  2  3  4  5  6
 7  8  9 10 11 12 13
14 15 16 17 18 19 20
21 22 23 24 25 26 27
28 29 30 31
```

APRIL
M T W T F S S
```
             1  2  3
 4  5  6  7  8  9 10
11 12 13 14 15 16 17
18 19 20 21 22 23 24
25 26 27 28 29 30
```

MAY
M T W T F S S
```
                   1
 2  3  4  5  6  7  8
 9 10 11 12 13 14 15
16 17 18 19 20 21 22
23 24 25 26 27 28 29
30 31
```

JUNE
M T W T F S S
```
       1  2  3  4  5
 6  7  8  9 10 11 12
13 14 15 16 17 18 19
20 21 22 23 24 25 26
27 28 29 30
```

JULY
M T W T F S S
```
             1  2  3
 4  5  6  7  8  9 10
11 12 13 14 15 16 17
18 19 20 21 22 23 24
25 26 27 28 29 30 31
```

AUGUST
M T W T F S S
```
 1  2  3  4  5  6  7
 8  9 10 11 12 13 14
15 16 17 18 19 20 21
22 23 24 25 26 27 28
29 30 31
```

SEPTEMBER
M T W T F S S
```
       1  2  3  4
 5  6  7  8  9 10 11
12 13 14 15 16 17 18
19 20 21 22 23 24 25
26 27 28 29 30
```

OCTOBER
M T W T F S S
```
                1  2
 3  4  5  6  7  8  9
10 11 12 13 14 15 16
17 18 19 20 21 22 23
24 25 26 27 28 29 30
31
```

NOVEMBER
M T W T F S S
```
    1  2  3  4  5  6
 7  8  9 10 11 12 13
14 15 16 17 18 19 20
21 22 23 24 25 26 27
28 29 30
```

DECEMBER
M T W T F S S
```
       1  2  3  4
 5  6  7  8  9 10 11
12 13 14 15 16 17 18
19 20 21 22 23 24 25
26 27 28 29 30 31
```

2017

JANUARY
M T W T F S S
```
                   1
 2  3  4  5  6  7  8
 9 10 11 12 13 14 15
16 17 18 19 20 21 22
23 24 25 26 27 28 29
30 31
```

FEBRUARY
M T W T F S S
```
    1  2  3  4  5
 6  7  8  9 10 11 12
13 14 15 16 17 18 19
20 21 22 23 24 25 26
27 28
```

MARCH
M T W T F S S
```
    1  2  3  4  5
 6  7  8  9 10 11 12
13 14 15 16 17 18 19
20 21 22 23 24 25 26
27 28 29 30 31
```

APRIL
M T W T F S S
```
                1  2
 3  4  5  6  7  8  9
10 11 12 13 14 15 16
17 18 19 20 21 22 23
24 25 26 27 28 29 30
```

MAY
M T W T F S S
```
 1  2  3  4  5  6  7
 8  9 10 11 12 13 14
15 16 17 18 19 20 21
22 23 24 25 26 27 28
29 30 31
```

JUNE
M T W T F S S
```
          1  2  3  4
 5  6  7  8  9 10 11
12 13 14 15 16 17 18
19 20 21 22 23 24 25
26 27 28 29 30
```

JULY
M T W T F S S
```
                1  2
 3  4  5  6  7  8  9
10 11 12 13 14 15 16
17 18 19 20 21 22 23
24 25 26 27 28 29 30
31
```

AUGUST
M T W T F S S
```
    1  2  3  4  5  6
 7  8  9 10 11 12 13
14 15 16 17 18 19 20
21 22 23 24 25 26 27
28 29 30 31
```

SEPTEMBER
M T W T F S S
```
             1  2  3
 4  5  6  7  8  9 10
11 12 13 14 15 16 17
18 19 20 21 22 23 24
25 26 27 28 29 30
```

OCTOBER
M T W T F S S
```
                   1
 2  3  4  5  6  7  8
 9 10 11 12 13 14 15
16 17 18 19 20 21 22
23 24 25 26 27 28 29
30 31
```

NOVEMBER
M T W T F S S
```
    1  2  3  4  5
 6  7  8  9 10 11 12
13 14 15 16 17 18 19
20 21 22 23 24 25 26
27 28 29 30
```

DECEMBER
M T W T F S S
```
             1  2  3
 4  5  6  7  8  9 10
11 12 13 14 15 16 17
18 19 20 21 22 23 24
25 26 27 28 29 30 31
```

ALICE & DINAH

INTRODUCTION

Alice's Adventures Under Ground by Lewis Carroll is perhaps the most famous of all the British Library's 19th-century literary manuscripts. It is Lewis Carroll's first version of the work later published as *Alice's Adventures in Wonderland* (1865).

Lewis Carroll was the pen name of Charles Lutwidge Dodgson, born 27 January 1832, died 14 January 1898, known especially for his children's books, which are distinguished as satire and as examples of verbal wit. Carroll invented his pen name by translating his first two names into the Latin 'Carolus Lodovicus' and then anglicising it into 'Lewis Carroll'.

The tale was first told by Carroll on 4 July 1862, to the three young daughters of Henry Liddell, Dean of Christ Church, Oxford, on a river boat trip. The children, especially Alice, adored the story and begged Carroll to write it down. It took him until February 1863 to write out the whole text, taking great pains to write in neat 'manuscript print', designed for the young Alice to read. Once the text was complete, Carroll began to add the illustrations, which give a charming impression of his own vision of Wonderland and its inhabitants.

The final 90-page manuscript was completed in September 1864, bound in green morocco leather and given to Alice on 26 November. Carroll's inscription read 'A Christmas Gift to a Dear Child, in Memory of a Summer Day'. The earlier text contains private Liddell family jokes and references, which were later removed from the expanded story.

Alice's Adventures Under Ground and *Alice's Adventures in Wonderland* differ in quite a few respects, most significantly in their length. *Alice's Adventures Under Ground* contains 12,715 words compared to *Alice's Adventures in Wonderland*, which was expanded by Carroll to 26,211. John Tenniel was commissioned to provide the original illustrations, several of which were based on Carroll's original sketches in the manuscript.

The illustrations herein celebrate the many editions published in the 150 years since *Alice's Adventures in Wonderland* was first published in 1865.

Alice and Dinah, illustration by Gwynedd M. Hudson published by Hodder and Stoughton, London, 1922. [YA.1997.b.4119]

DECEMBER & JANUARY

28 Monday   Holiday, UK, Republic of Ireland, Canada,
Australia and New Zealand

29 Tuesday

30 Wednesday

31 Thursday   New Year's Eve

1 Friday   New Year's Day
Holiday, UK, Republic of Ireland, Canada,
USA, Australia and New Zealand

2 Saturday   *Last Quarter*
Holiday, Scotland and New Zealand

3 Sunday

The Pool of Tears, **Alice swims surrounded by various animals**, illustration by Arthur Rackham,
London, 1907. [K.T.C.105.b.1.]

JANUARY

4 Monday

5 Tuesday

6 Wednesday   Epiphany

7 Thursday

8 Friday

Illuminated letter C with Alice and the White Rabbit, illustration by Gwynedd M. Hudson
London, 1922. [YA.1997.b.4119]

9 Saturday

SOCCER GAME : 4:00

movie : 5:30

Daddy's @ 4-Star Theater
Home

10 Sunday

New Moon

---

11 Monday   read: Emancipation Proclamation ☐

☐ subordinate clauses worksheet
☐ ss reading and qs
☐ ss classwork...
☐ read ms. charm's Hiaku...

---

12 Tuesday   come in early @ 7:30 for math lab

☒ La Exam

---

13 Wednesday

---

14 Thursday

---

15 Friday

---

16 Saturday   *First Quarter*

---

17 Sunday

Alice and the White Rabbit, illustration by Arthur Rackham, London, 1907. [K.T.C.105.b.1.]

JANUARY

---

18 Monday
Holiday, USA (Martin Luther King Jnr Day)

---

19 Tuesday

---

20 Wednesday

---

21 Thursday

---

22 Friday

---

23 Saturday

---

24 Sunday
Full Moon

Alice meets the Blue Caterpillar, illustration by Sir John Tenniel, London, 1890. [Cup.410.g.74]

JANUARY

25 Monday

26 Tuesday

Holiday, Australia (Australia Day)

27 Wednesday

28 Thursday

29 Friday

30 Saturday

31 Sunday

Alice Through the Looking Glass, illustration by Sir John Tenniel, London, 1940.

FEBRUARY

1 Monday   *Last Quarter*

2 Tuesday

3 Wednesday

4 Thursday

5 Friday

6 Saturday

Accession of Queen Elizabeth II
Holiday, New Zealand
(Waitangi Day)

7 Sunday

Illustrations by Sir John Tenniel, London, 1865. [C.59.g.11]

FEBRUARY

8 Monday

New Moon
Chinese New Year

---

9 Tuesday

Shrove Tuesday

---

10 Wednesday

Ash Wednesday

---

11 Thursday

---

12 Friday

---

13 Saturday

---

14 Sunday

Valentine's Day

Alice and the Queen of Hearts, illustration by Sir John Tenniel published by Macmillan & Co., London, 1890. [Cup.410.g.74]

FEBRUARY

15 Monday

First Quarter
Holiday, USA (Presidents' Day)

16 Tuesday

17 Wednesday

18 Thursday

19 Friday

Illuminated letter T with Alice eating from a mushroom, illustration by Gwynedd M. Hudson, London, 1922. [YA.1997.b.4119]

20 Saturday

21 Sunday

FEBRUARY

22 Monday   *Full Moon*

23 Tuesday

24 Wednesday

25 Thursday

26 Friday

27 Saturday

28 Sunday

The White Rabbit, illustration by Sir John Tenniel, London, 1890. [Cup.410.g.74]

"A CAUCUS-RACE AND A LONG TALE."

CHAPTER III.

HEY were indeed a queer-looking party that assembled on the bank— the birds with draggled feathers, the animals with their fur clinging close to them, and all dripping wet, cross, and uncomfortable.

The first question, of course, was, how to get dry again: they had a consultation about this, and after a few minutes it seemed quite natural to Alice to find herself talking familiarly with them, as if she had known them all her life. Indeed, she had quite a long argument with the Lory, who at last turned sulky, and would only say, "I am older than you, and must know better;" and this Alice would not allow without knowing how old it

29 Monday

1 Tuesday

Last Quarter
St David's Day

2 Wednesday

3 Thursday

4 Friday

5 Saturday

6 Sunday

Mother's Day
UK and Republic of Ireland

An illustrated page by Gwynedd M. Hudson, London, 1922. [YA.1997.b.4119]

MARCH

7 Monday

8 Tuesday

9 Wednesday   *New Moon*

10 Thursday

11 Friday

12 Saturday

13 Sunday

Alice talking to the Blue Caterpillar, illustration by Gwynedd M. Hudson, London, 1922.
[YA.1997.b.4119]

Gwynedd.M.Hudson

MARCH

14 Monday   Commonwealth Day

15 Tuesday   *First Quarter*

16 Wednesday

17 Thursday   St. Patrick's Day
Holiday, Northern Ireland
and Republic of Ireland

18 Friday

elbow against the door, and the other arm curled round her head. Still she went on growing, and, as a last resource, she put one arm out of the window, and one foot up the chimney, and said to herself, "Now I can do no more, whatever happens. What *will* become of me?"

Luckily for Alice, the little magic bottle had now had its full effect, and she grew no larger : still it was very uncomfortable, and as there seemed to be no sort of chance of her ever

19 Saturday

20 Sunday
Spring Equinox
Palm Sunday

Illustrations by Sir John Tenniel, London, 1865.
[C.59.g.11]

MARCH

21 Monday

22 Tuesday

23 Wednesday   *Full Moon*

24 Thursday   Maundy Thursday

25 Friday   Good Friday
                                                           Holiday, UK, Canada,
                                                       Australia and New Zealand

26 Saturday   Holiday Australia (Easter Saturday)

27 Sunday   Easter Sunday
                                                      British Summer Time begins

The White Rabbit, illustration by Gwynedd M. Hudson, London, 1922. [YA.1997.b.4119]

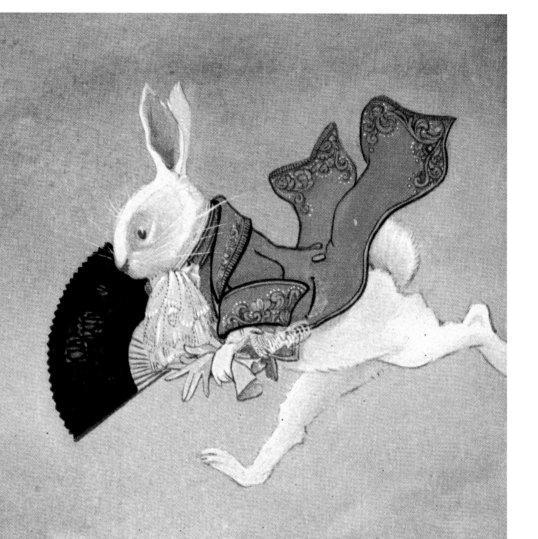

Gwynedd. M. Hudson.

28 Monday

Easter Monday
Holiday UK (exc. Scotland), Republic of Ireland,
Australia and New Zealand

29 Tuesday

30 Wednesday

31 Thursday

Last Quarter

1 Friday

2 Saturday

3 Sunday

The Mad Hatter and the March Hare, illustration by Gwynedd M. Hudson, London, 1922.
[YA.1997.b.4119]

APRIL

4 Monday

5 Tuesday

6 Wednesday

7 Thursday   *New Moon*

8 Friday

9 Saturday

10 Sunday

The front cover of *Alice's Adventures in Wonderland,* illustration by Arthur Rackham, London, 1907.
[K.T.C.105.b.1.]

ALICE'S ADVENTURES IN WONDERLAND

By LEWIS CARROLL

"Alice"

ILLUSTRATED BY ARTHUR RACKHAM

APRIL

11 Monday

12 Tuesday

13 Wednesday

14 Thursday   *Fisrt Quarter*

15 Friday

16 Saturday

17 Sunday

Alice and the Duchess playing croquet, illustration by Sir John Tenniel, London, 1890.
[Cup.410.g.74]

APRIL

18 Monday

19 Tuesday

20 Wednesday

21 Thursday   Birthday of Queen Elizabeth II

22 Friday   *Full Moon*

The Mad Hatter and the March Hare, illustration by Gwynedd M. Hudson, London, 1922.
[YA.1997.b.4119]

23 Saturday

24 Sunday

APRIL & MAY

25 Monday

Anzac Day
Holiday, Australia and New Zealand

26 Tuesday

27 Wednesday

28 Thursday

29 Friday

30 Saturday

Last Quarter

1 Sunday

Alice by the Door in the Tree, illustration by Charles Lutwidge Dodgson (Lewis Carroll) 1862-1864. [Add. 46700]

MAY

2 Monday

Early Spring Bank Holiday,
UK and Republic of Ireland

3 Tuesday

4 Wednesday

5 Thursday

Ascension Day

6 Friday

New Moon

7 Saturday

8 Sunday

Mother's Day
USA and Canada

Alice and the Duchess during a game of croquet, illustration by Gwynedd M. Hudson, London, 1922. [YA.1997.b.4119]

MAY

9 Monday

10 Tuesday

11 Wednesday

12 Thursday

13 Friday   *First Quarter*

Alice and the Dodo, The Caucus-Race, illustration by Sir John Tenniel, London, 1890. [Cup.410.g.74]

14 Saturday

15 Sunday   Whit Sunday

16 Monday

17 Tuesday

18 Wednesday

19 Thursday

20 Friday

21 Saturday   *Full Moon*

22 Sunday   Trinity Sunday

Alice and the Pack of Playing Cards, illustration by Arthur Rackham, London, 1907.
[K.T.C.105.b.1.]

MAY

23 Monday	Victoria Day Holiday, Canada

24 Tuesday	

25 Wednesday	

26 Thursday	Corpus Christi

27 Friday	

28 Saturday	

29 Sunday	*Last Quarter*

Inspecting the Tarts, illustration by Sir John Tenniel, London, 1890. [Cup.410.g.74]

DOWN THE RABBIT-HOLE

LICE was beginning to get very tired of sitting by her sister on the bank, and of having nothing to do: once or twice she had peeped into the book her sister was reading, but it had no pictures or conversations in it, " and what is the use of a book," thought Alice, " without pictures or conversations ? "

So she was considering in her own mind (as well as she could, for the hot day made her feel very sleepy and stupid) whether the pleasure of making a daisy-chain would be worth the trouble of getting up and picking the daisies, when suddenly a White Rabbit with pink eyes ran close by her.

There was nothing so *very* remarkable in that; nor did Alice think it so *very* much out

1

MAY & JUNE

30 Monday

Spring Bank Holiday
UK and Republic of Ireland

31 Tuesday

1 Wednesday

2 Thursday

Coronation Day

3 Friday

4 Saturday

5 Sunday

New Moon

An illustrated page by Gwynedd M. Hudson, London, 1922. [YA.1997.b.4119]

JUNE

6 Monday

---

7 Tuesday   First day of Ramadan
                                          (subject to sighting of the moon)

8 Wednesday

---

9 Thursday

10 Friday

---

11 Saturday

The Queen's Official Birthday
*Date subject to confirmation

12 Sunday

First Quarter
Feast of Weeks (Shavuot)

Illustrations by Arthur Rackham, London, 1907.
[K.T.C.105.b.1.]

JUNE

---

13 Monday

---

14 Tuesday

---

15 Wednesday

---

16 Thursday

---

17 Friday

---

18 Saturday

---

19 Sunday

Father's Day
UK, Republic of Ireland, USA and Canada

Two Guinea Pigs Dressed as Maids, illustration by Gwynedd M. Hudson, London, 1922.
[YA.1997.b.4119]

JUNE

20 Monday

Full Moon
Summer Solstice (summer begins)

21 Tuesday

22 Wednesday

23 Thursday

24 Friday

25 Saturday

26 Sunday

Trial of the Knave of Hearts, illustration by Charles Lutwidge Dodgson (Lewis Carroll) 1862-1864.
[Add. 46700]

JUNE & JULY

27 Monday — *Last Quarter*

28 Tuesday

29 Wednesday

30 Thursday

1 Friday — Holiday, Canada (Canada Day)

2 Saturday

3 Sunday

Mock Turtle and Gryphon, illustration by Sir John Tenniel, London, 1890. [Cup.410.g.74]

JULY

---

4 Monday

---

5 Tuesday

Eid al-Fitr (end of Ramadan)
(subject to sighting of the moon)

---

6 Wednesday

---

7 Thursday

---

8 Friday

---

9 Saturday

---

10 Sunday

The Queen of Hearts Shouting at the Executioner, illustration by Gwynedd M. Hudson, London, 1922. [YA.1997.b.4119]

JULY

---

11 Monday

---

12 Tuesday

First Quarter
Holiday, Northern Ireland (Battle of the Boyne)

---

13 Wednesday

---

14 Thursday

---

15 Friday

St. Swithin's Day

---

16 Saturday

---

17 Sunday

The Shower of Cards, illustration by Sir John Tenniel, London, 1890. [Cup.410.g.74]

JULY

18 Monday

19 Tuesday   *Full Moon*

20 Wednesday

21 Thursday

22 Friday

23 Saturday

24 Sunday

The King and Queen of Hearts upon their Throne at Court, illustration by Gwynedd M. Hudson, London, 1922. [YA.1997.b.4119]

JULY

---

25 Monday

---

26 Tuesday   *Last Quarter*

---

27 Wednesday

---

28 Thursday

29 Friday

30 Saturday

31 Sunday

Illustrations by Sir John Tenniel, London, 1865. [C.59.g.11]

AUGUST

1 Monday   Holiday, Scotland and Republic of Ireland

2 Tuesday   *New Moon*

3 Wednesday

4 Thursday

5 Friday

6 Saturday

7 Sunday

The Playing Cards, illustration by Sir John Tenniel, London, 1890. [Cup.410.g.74]

AUGUST

8 Monday

9 Tuesday

10 Wednesday   *First Quarter*

11 Thursday

12 Friday

13 Saturday

14 Sunday

Alice with the Pig-Baby, illustration by Arthur Rackham, London, 1907. [K.T.C.105.b.1.]

AUGUST

15 Monday

16 Tuesday

17 Wednesday

18 Thursday   *Full Moon*

19 Friday

20 Saturday

21 Sunday

Alice and the Shower of Cards, illustration by Gwynedd M. Hudson, London, 1922. [YA.1997.b.4119]

AUGUST

22 Monday

23 Tuesday

24 Wednesday

25 Thursday   *Last Quarter*

26 Friday

27 Saturday

28 Sunday

Alice in a Kitchen with the Duchess, a Cook and the Cheshire Cat, illustration by
Arthur Rackham, London, 1907. [K.T.C.105.b.1.]

AUGUST & SEPTEMBER

29 Monday Holiday, UK (exc. Scotland)

---

30 Tuesday

---

31 Wednesday

---

1 Thursday *New Moon*

---

2 Friday

Shrunken Alice and the Puppy by a Giant Thistle, illustration by Gwynedd M. Hudson, London, 1922. [YA.1997.b.4119]

3 Saturday

---

4 Sunday
Father's Day,
Australia and New Zealand

SEPTEMBER

---

5 Monday

---

6 Tuesday

---

7 Wednesday

---

8 Thursday

---

9 Friday *First Quarter*

---

10 Saturday

---

11 Sunday

Alice and the Pig-Baby, illustration by Sir John Tenniel, London, 1890. [Cup.410.g.74]

SEPTEMBER

12 Monday

13 Tuesday

14 Wednesday

15 Thursday

16 Friday   *Full Moon*

Eat Me, illustration by Gwynedd M. Hudson, London, 1922. [YA.1997.b.4119]

17 Saturday

18 Sunday

19 Monday

20 Tuesday

21 Wednesday

22 Thursday   Autumnal Equinox (Autumn begins)

23 Friday   *Last Quarter*

24 Saturday

25 Sunday

Alice with the Gryphon and the Mock Turtle, illustration by Arthur Rackham, London, 1907. [K.T.C.105.b.1.]

SEPTEMBER & OCTOBER

26 Monday

27 Tuesday

28 Wednesday

29 Thursday   Michaelmas Day

30 Friday

1 Saturday   *New Moon*

2 Sunday

Alice and the Cheshire Cat, illustration by Sir John Tenniel, London, 1890. [Cup.410.g.74]

And that reminds me. There's a little lesson I want to teach *you*, while we're looking at this picture of Alice and the Cat. Now don't be in a bad temper about it, my dear Child! It's a very *little* lesson indeed!

Do you see that Fox-Glove growing close to the tree? And do you know why it's called a *Fox*-Glove? Perhaps you

OCTOBER

3 Monday

Jewish New Year (Rosh Hashanah)
and Islamic New Year

4 Tuesday

5 Wednesday

6 Thursday

7 Friday

8 Saturday

9 Sunday

First Quarter

Alice and the Duchess, illustration by Gwynedd M. Hudson, London, 1922. [YA.1997.b.4119]

OCTOBER

10 Monday

11 Tuesday

12 Wednesday

Day of Atonement
(Yom Kippur)

13 Thursday

14 Friday

15 Saturday

16 Sunday   *Full Moon*

OCTOBER

17 Monday   First day of Tabernacles (Sukkot)

18 Tuesday

19 Wednesday

20 Thursday

21 Friday

22 Saturday   *Last Quarter*

23 Sunday

Alice and the Caterpillar, illustration by Arthur Rackham, London, 1907. [K.T.C.105.b.1.]

ALICE'S·ADVENTURES
IN·WONDERLAND
BY·LEWIS·CARROLL
ILLUSTRATED·BY
ARTHUR·RACKHAM

WITH A PROEM BY AUSTIN DOBSON

LONDON·WILLIAM·HEINEMANN
NEW·YORK·DOUBLEDAY·PAGE·&·C°

OCTOBER

24 Monday

Holiday, New Zealand (Labour Day)

25 Tuesday

26 Wednesday

27 Thursday

28 Friday

29 Saturday

30 Sunday

New Moon
British Summer Time ends

Illustrations by Arthur Rackham, London, 1907. [K.T.C.105.b.1.]

OCTOBER & NOVEMBER

31 Monday   Halloween

1 Tuesday   All Saints' Day

2 Wednesday

3 Thursday

4 Friday

Alice, illustration by Gwynedd M. Hudson, London, 1922. [YA.1997.b.4119]

5 Saturday   Guy Fawkes

6 Sunday

NOVEMBER

---

7 Monday   *First Quarter*

---

8 Tuesday

---

9 Wednesday

---

10 Thursday

---

11 Friday   Holiday, USA (Veterans' Day)
                                    and Canada (Remembrance Day)

---

12 Saturday

---

13 Sunday   Remembrance Sunday

Alice Dancing with the Mock Turtle and the Gryphon, illustration by Gwynedd M. Hudson, London, 1922. [YA.1997.b.4119]

NOVEMBER

14 Monday

15 Tuesday

16 Wednesday

17 Thursday

18 Friday

19 Saturday

20 Sunday

Dash the Puppy, illustration by Sir John Tenniel, London, 1890. [Cup.410.g.74]

NOVEMBER

21 Monday   *Last Quarter*

22 Tuesday

23 Wednesday

24 Thursday   Holiday, USA (Thanksgiving)

25 Friday

26 Saturday

27 Sunday   First Sunday in Advent

The Mad Hatter's Tea Party, illustration by Arthur Rackham, London, 1907. [K.T.C.105.b.1.]

NOVEMBER & DECEMBER

---

28 Monday

---

29 Tuesday   *New Moon*

---

30 Wednesday   St. Andrew's Day

---

1 Thursday

---

2 Friday

The Mad Hatter's Tea Party, illustration by Sir John Tenniel, London, 1890. [Cup.410.g.74]

DECEMBER

5 Monday

6 Tuesday

7 Wednesday   *First Quarter*

8 Thursday

9 Friday

10 Saturday

11 Sunday

Alice at the Trial, illustration by Sir John Tenniel, London, 1890. [Cup.410.g.74]

DECEMBER

12 Monday

13 Tuesday

14 Wednesday   *Full Moon*

15 Thursday

16 Friday

Beautiful Soup! illustration by Gwynedd M. Hudson, London, 1922. [YA.1997.b.4119]

17 Saturday

18 Sunday

DECEMBER

19 Monday

---

20 Tuesday   Winter Solstice (Winter begins)

---

21 Wednesday   *Last Quarter*

---

22 Thursday

---

23 Friday

---

24 Saturday   Christmas Eve
                                                        Hanukkah begins

---

25 Sunday   Christmas Day

The Queen of Hearts, illustration by Arthur Rackham, London, 1907. [K.T.C.105.b.1.]

DECEMBER & JANUARY

---

26 Monday

Holiday, UK, Republic of Ireland, Canada,
Australia and New Zealand
Boxing Day (St. Stephen's Day)

---

27 Tuesday

Holiday, UK, Republic of Ireland, USA, Canada,
Australia and New Zealand

---

28 Wednesday

---

29 Thursday

New Moon

---

30 Friday

---

31 Saturday

New Year's Eve

---

1 Sunday

New Year's Day
Holiday, UK, Republic of Ireland, USA, Canada,
Australia and New Zealand

Alice as a Serpent Talking to a Pigeon, illustration by Arthur Rackham, London, 1907.
[K.T.C.105.b.1.]

JANUARY 2017

2 Monday   Holiday, Scotland and New Zealand

3 Tuesday

4 Wednesday

5 Thursday

6 Friday   Epiphany

7 Saturday

8 Sunday